Made in the USA
Coppell, TX
03 June 2024

33056192R00073